DEVOTIONAL

THE

Christmas Promise

DEVOTIONAL

A Journey from Cradle to Crown

MARGIE WILLIAMSON

NEW HOPE®
PUBLISHERS
Imprint of Iron Stream Media

New Hope® Publishers
100 Missionary Ridge
Birmingham, AL 35242
NewHopePublishers.com
An imprint of Iron Stream Media
IronStreamMedia.com

ISBN-13: 978-1-56309-388-3
Ebook ISBN 13: 978-1-56309-393-7

1 2 3 4 5—24 23 22 21 20

Contents

Jesus the Boy
Key Passage–Luke 2:41

Jesus the Man
Key Passage–Philippians 2:7

Jesus the Messiah
Key Passage–Mark 1:11

Jesus the Savior and Redeemer
Key Passage–Matthew 34:20

God's Amazing Plan

We usually study the birth of Christ at Advent as a single, glorious event. Everything about the Advent story pulls at our emotions: the young virgin who was willing to do whatever God wanted of her; the betrothed husband who put aside cultural traditions to humbly be used by God; the quiet, humble birth in a borrowed stable; and the glorious proclamation of the birth by an army of God's angels to the shepherds nearby. It's a wonderful story.

But Advent is so much more than that. Advent is one part of God's amazing plan for His people. This Advent season, rejoice in the birth of God's Son as you also look at the bigger picture—God's plan to bring salvation and restoration through His Son—by taking a journey from the cradle to the crown.

God's Plan

Key Passage
Galatians 4:4–6

Day 1

In the Beginning

> But when the fullness of time had come, God
> sent forth his Son, born of woman, born under
> the law, to redeem those who were under the
> law, so that we might receive adoption as sons.
> —Galatians 4:4–5

In the beginning.... Those are powerful words. We celebrate beginnings—new life, new commitments, new opportunities—because beginnings open up a world of possibilities for us. The Bible begins with those words and includes one more—*in the beginning, God.* The account in Genesis is more than just about creation—it's about the Creator. And the beginning of Genesis is not about God's beginning because He is eternal. He was before the world and He will be forever. God, the Creator, began with nothing but a plan. From nothing, He created something and gave it form and structure. He created the world and the universe to operate in order, not chaos. His creation was not a spur of the moment thing—it was planned to perfection. In His time, He has created, He has loved, He has redeemed, and He waits with anticipation for the time when all His plans will finally be fulfilled.

Read Galatians 4:4–7. Paul also reflected on God the Creator's plan. The words, *when the fullness of time had come,* are more than a statement of taking the next step of a plan. The Greek word for "fullness" can be understood as completion (doing what it takes to finish something) or repleteness (having something in abundance). God waited for the right time, the perfect time, before He sent His Son to the world. This was planned from the beginning and was intentional. It couldn't have been without pain and sacrifice on His part. God sent His one and only Son, the unique Son of God, to become man, to love us as God already loves us, and to suffer extraordinarily for us so we could accept God's grace. In God's plan and in His timing, He sent His Son to take on our sin as His own.

Reflect on the fact that God sent His only Son for you. What does His willingness to sacrifice His own Son teach you about how God feels about you?

Think about God's plan in the beginning. How do you see Advent as part of God's overall plan?

As you pray, confess your confidence in the fullness of God's plan through the birth of Jesus, and thank Him that through His birth, Jesus has redeemed you and restored you to His Father.

Day 2

God Declared Long Ago

I declared them to you from of old, before they came to pass I announced them to you, . . . From this time forth I announce to you new things, hidden things that you have not known.—Isaiah 48:5–6

By definition, a prophecy is a declaration about something that will one day happen. Prophetic statements abound in the Old Testament, even in books like Genesis, Exodus, Leviticus, Deuteronomy, and Psalms, as well as the books of prophecy, such as Isaiah, Jeremiah, Ezekiel, Daniel, Micah, and Zephaniah. In fact, biblical scholars have identified more than 1,200 prophecies in the Old Testament alone. That's 1,200 times in the Old Testament that God revealed more details about His plan, His timing, and the coming of His Son. That's also 1,200 times that God's plan was woven into the very fiber of the Old Testament. The huge number of prophecies also points us to God's consistency. God is eternal, consistent, and unchanging. His plan has never wavered. And He has used opportunity after opportunity to make sure the world knew of His plan.

Read Isaiah 48:3–6. The people of Israel had heard God's promises for centuries, and yet they were unfaithful to Him. Through Isaiah, God proclaimed that they had earned His wrath and would feel His judgment. God's people had already seen His mighty works. They watched Him free them from Egypt. They stood on the banks of the Red Sea and watched Him part it so they could escape the coming Egyptian army. They followed His very presence across the wilderness, and they experienced victory after victory in the Promised Land. In spite of all they had witnessed, they wouldn't trust Him fully or obey Him completely. In Isaiah 48, God announced that His message for them contained new things, and He was ready to reveal more of what was to come. In fact, the book of Isaiah contains at least fifteen prophecies that were just about the Messiah.

Most of the people of Israel were never able to comprehend what God was going to do. Instead, they chose to remain in disobedience and faced the consequences. Even in judgment, however, God promised hope—hope that would come to be in the birth of His Son.

Imagine the Old Testament visually as a finely woven piece of linen. What does that illustration suggest about God and His Word?

What does the consistency of the message of the Old Testament mean in your understanding of the New Testament?

As you pray, praise God for who He is—eternal, loving, forgiving, merciful, and unchangeable.

Day 3

Behold, My Servant

> Behold my servant, whom I uphold, my cho-
> sen, in whom my soul delights; I have put my
> Spirit upon him; he will bring forth justice to
> the nations.—Isaiah 42:1

God called prophets to be His voice to His people. They
spoke the words God told them to speak, and in some cas-
es, such as the prophet Ezekiel, they acted out His message
as He directed. When you read the major prophets (Isaiah,
Jeremiah, Ezekiel), you'll see the relationship between them
and God. He directed; they obeyed. He spoke; they retold.
He planned; they proclaimed the details. Part of what they
proclaimed was that there was One who would come who
would be a prophet, but He would be more than a prophet.
This One would be a priest, but He would be more than a
priest. This One would come with the unique identity of
being God's Son and with the unique mission of being the
Messiah.

Read Luke 42:1–4. God described this One who was to
come to Isaiah. This One would be God's servant, One spe-
cifically chosen by God, and One that cost God dearly. This
One would reveal God in everything He did, bringing justice to the world in His gentleness, care and healing in His
compassion, and strength in His calmness. This One would

be unlike any servant the people had ever seen before. He would work ceaselessly and without discouragement, even when the people wouldn't listen, until He fulfilled His mission of bringing justice on earth.

We know that the One is Jesus. He came not only to reveal God to the world but also to be a part of the world Himself. He conducted Himself in gentleness, and yet He showed strength as He moved toward the cross. His mission never changed; His obedience never wavered.

Jesus was not the typical servant. He was committed to God's plan, and it showed in His attitude and His demeanor. He came down from heaven to walk as we walk and live as we live. He endured the people's rejection and never faltered. He remained caring, patient, and focused. And, God took great delight in His Son and His Servant.

What did it cost God to send His Son to be the Servant of mankind?

Think of examples in scripture when Jesus demonstrated the characteristics of gentleness, strength, compassion, and patience. How do these characteristics portray the character of God?

As you pray, ask God to make you aware of when your attitude and demeanor fall short of bringing Him glory.

Day 4

No Form of Majesty

For he grew up before him like a young plant,
and like a root out of dry ground; he had no
form or majesty that we should look at him,
and no beauty that we should desire him.
—Isaiah 53:2

Jesus' life was one of humble circumstances. He was born
in a stable; He was a refugee in Egypt; His father was a poor
carpenter; He had no dwelling of His own; He died a pauper. None of these suggest His was the life of a King, much
less the long-awaited Messiah. Isaiah 53 is an often-used
passage of scripture at Easter because it speaks of the suffering of the Son of God in our place. But Isaiah 53 also provides an interesting picture of Jesus' life—of how He looked
and how He was treated.

Read Isaiah 53:1–3. Remember that Isaiah's prophecy
was given 700 years before the birth of Jesus. Yet the details
are specific. Isaiah first identified Jesus as "the arm of the
Lord." That phrase is used throughout the Old Testament
to refer to God's power and strength. From that beginning,
Isaiah described Jesus in terms that did not call up visions
of strength and power. Jesus would grow up naturally as a
child, but He would be like a tender plant, seemingly weak
or fragile. Not only that, Jesus would look average. He would

look like everyone else. Isaiah didn't say Jesus would be ugly, but that Jesus would not have the physical attractiveness that would draw people to Him. On the other hand, His average looks would have allowed Him to relate to all people—the poor, the rejected, the suffering, the weak, the unloved, and the unspectacular.

Despite His desire to be the Savior for all people, Jesus would be despised and rejected by the very people He had come to save. He would be made to suffer. He would be the person that people turned away from because they didn't value Him.

God chose for His Son to look average on earth. Do you think His appearance helped His ministry or hindered it? Why?

Jesus faced total rejection by those He came to serve. What kind of pain do you think He experienced through this rejection?

As you pray, express your gratefulness for all the pain and rejection that Jesus willingly took on for you.

Day 5

Only God

And he will go before him in the spirit and
power of Elijah, to turn the hearts of the fa-
thers to the children, and the disobedient to
the wisdom of the just, to make ready for the
Lord a people prepared.—Luke 1:17

Many scholars see John the Baptist as the final Old Testament prophet. He is definitely the bridge that connects the
Old Testament to the New and proclaims the coming of Jesus as the fulfillment of the Old Testament prophecies. His
life and mission were indelibly connected to Jesus. John was
tied to Jesus by family blood. He was called with the mission
of preparing Israel for the coming Messiah. And, in compar-
ison, John the Baptist as a prophet showed that Jesus was
more than that.

God also demonstrated the importance of John the
Baptist's role by orchestrating the events surrounding his
birth.

Read Luke 1:8–20. Zechariah and Elizabeth's story is
much like Abram and Sarai's in Genesis. They desperate-
ly wanted a child but were far past childbearing years and
had given up all hope. Zechariah served as one of the temple priests, serving at the temple twice a year for a week.
The most holy assignment the priests had was to keep the

incense within the temple burning, so every morning, lots were cast to see who would take care of that task. There were so many priests in Israel that many were never chosen. Once chosen, a priest could never again fulfill that function. Casting lots was used in both the Old and the New Testaments to determine God's will.

Being chosen would have been an incredibly divine moment for Zechariah. He had been given the opportunity to come into the very presence of God. Then the Lord's archangel Gabriel appeared with the news that Zechariah and his wife would have a child, stunning Zechariah in the process. Zechariah asked the same question Abram had asked: How can this be? The answer was obvious—only God could make that happen. Only God could have chosen this baby to be the one to prepare the world for the work of His Own Son. Only God has an army of angels to do His bidding. Only God can make the seemingly impossible happen.

How does John the Baptist's assignment demonstrate God's plan?

God used supernatural ways to communicate with Zechariah. Have you seen God's supernatural power in your life? How?

As you pray, thank God for the things you see and understand, and those you don't.

Day 6

Generations in the Lord

So all the generations from Abraham to
David were fourteen generations, and from
David to the deportation to Babylon four-
teen generations, and from the deportation to
Babylon to the Christ fourteen generations.
—Matthew 1:17

There is possibly no simpler way of seeing God's plan than
in Matthew 1:1–17. Through the generations that began
with God's covenant agreement with Abraham in Genesis,
Matthew outlined how God had brought His plan to completion—He had done it one generation after another of
people who belonged to Him and with whom He had a covenant relationship. As Matthew recorded the genealogy of
Jesus' lineage, he also emphasized keys about the character
and nature of God.

Read Matthew 1:1-17. Matthew began with Abraham,
not Adam, because it was with Abraham that God made His
covenant. God promised that He would give Abraham the
land, the descendants, and His blessing. And God promised
that Abraham would be a blessing (Gen. 12:1–3). Matthew
documented the beginning of God's relationship with the
Jews through Abraham and showed that God had faithfully
kept His promises to them throughout their history.

Interestingly, Matthew included the names of four women in the genealogy—Rahab, Ruth, Tamar, and Bathsheba. That's curious because Jews trace their lineage through the men. Notice that Rahab, a Canaanite, and Ruth, a Moabite, were both foreigners. Two of the women were known for their sin. Tamar presented herself as a prostitute to Judah, the father of her first two husbands, and became pregnant. By tricking Judah, she became the mother of Perez and Zerah (Gen. 38). Bathsheba, a married woman, had a baby with King David. Despite their faults, or possibly because of their faults, they are listed in Jesus' genealogy. God's mercy and grace did more than cover their sin; it made them part of His people.

Matthew also showed the order and symmetry of God's plan. Fourteen generations from Abraham to David, fourteen generations from David to Josiah, and fourteen generations from Jechoniah to Joseph show God's plan is in the details. He is a God of order, not confusion, and of grace and forgiveness. It's all there in the genealogy.

What speaks to you most about God's character in these verses?

How have you experienced God's order and grace?

As you pray, thank God for who He is, for what He has done in the past, and for what He will do in the future.

Jesus the Babe

Key Passage
Isaiah 9:6

Day 7

The Promise of the Newborn Babe

For to us a child is born, to us a son is given; and the government shall be upon his shoulder, and his name shall be called Wonderful Counselor, Mighty God, Everlasting Father, Prince of Peace.—Isaiah 9:6

If you have been able to hold a newborn baby, you understand the feeling of seeing God's perfection at work. Newborns are so beautiful (especially to their parents) in their completeness, with fingers that can already grasp, and with the ability to suckle, to breathe, to see, to hear. It's hard to look at a newborn and not praise God for the way He so wondrously made us. God's hand in creation is seen as we look on and hold that newborn babe. Yet God's creation is also seen internally. Psalm 139:13 states, "For you formed my inward parts; you knitted me together in my mother's womb." And in Jeremiah 1:5, God told Jeremiah, "Before I formed you in the womb I knew you, and before you were born I consecrated you; I appointed you a prophet to the nations."

Read Isaiah 9:1–7. The people of the Northern Kingdom of Israel had turned away from God and were under constant military siege from Assyria. In what seemed to be a hopeless situation, God used Isaiah to share a message of hope: one day, peace would come at the hand of a great king, King Jesus. Isaiah's message was simple. He told them that God knew they were in distress, and that they needed to hold on because a better day was coming (vv. 1–3). God promised to redeem the people in a way unlike anything they had experienced—He promised to destroy their enemies and to bring them peace (vv. 4–5). God promised this peace through the birth of His only Son, Jesus, who would come to us as a newborn babe (Isaiah 9:6–7).

Imagine looking upon the newborn Christ Child. How would that experience compare with your experiences with newborns?

When you consider the care with which God designed us, is it any wonder that He chose to send His Son to us as a newborn babe?

As you pray, thank Him that He loved you before you were even formed, just as He did His Son, and praise Him that He has created you in such a magnificent process.

Day 8

Divine Understanding

> And the angel said to her, "Do not be afraid,
> Mary, for you have found favor with God. And
> behold, you will conceive in your womb and
> bear a son, and you shall call his name Jesus.
> —Luke 1:30–31

Have you ever wondered who Mary had been before she was chosen to be the mother of God's Son? Interestingly, a few things can be drawn from scripture. First, Mary was young, possibly as young as twelve or as old as fifteen or sixteen. That's based on the fact that she was already betrothed to Joseph. Second, she lived in Nazareth because that's where the angel Gabriel visited her.

Read Luke 1:26–38. Notice that in verse 29, Mary didn't tremble in fear before the angel. She may have been the only person in scripture who was not afraid when coming face to face with an angel of the Lord. She only wondered what was going on. Plus, in verse 34, she had the temerity to question the angel about how all he said would come about. For a young girl, that boldness speaks to her character and her faith. In verse 38, Mary acknowledged herself as God's servant and committed herself to obedience. That, too, is an extraordinary statement of faith.

Possibly the most distinct clues are found in *The Magnificat*, Mary's song of praise in response to what God had chosen her to do (Luke 1:46–55). In verses 48–49, Mary said, "For behold, from now on all generations will call me blessed; for he who is mighty has done great things for me." What an exceptional statement of understanding the big picture of what God asked of her, and what a moment of prophecy about her own life! Her discernment could only have been divinely given. Also, Mary knew the Old Testament, especially biblical prophecies. In *The Magnificat*, Mary prayed words that seem to reflect Hannah's prayer in 1 Samuel 2:1–10.

Why do you think so little information about Mary's background is provided in scripture?

Without the background information, what do you think Luke wanted us to know about Mary?

Read *The Magnificat* and reflect on how Mary's words were divinely inspired. As you pray, ask God to help you see how He is at work in your life as clearly as Mary was able to see Him in her life.

Day 9

The Rhythm of Life

When Joseph woke from sleep, he did as the
angel of the Lord commanded him: he took
his wife, but knew her not until she had given
birth to a son. And he called his name Jesus.
—Matthew 1:24–25

God's created world has rhythm to it. There's the changing
of seasons that constantly renews the sustaining life on the
planet. There's the rhythm of the oceans and the way the
tides are impacted by the moon. There's the rhythm in ma-
turing of our own beings—we grow and develop in rhythm
with where we are in age and development. Life has rhythm.

The Jewish faith has rhythms as well—set out by the
laws God gave their ancestors. Those rhythms set the way
they eat, the way they worship, and the way they raise their
families. And for Joseph in the first century, those rhythms
set his betrothal, his engagement, and his marriage. He
knew what to expect and how to act. But Joseph was also
from the line of David, and he knew the Old Testament
scripture. Would he not also have known the prophecies
about the birth of the Messiah from his own lineage (Isaiah
11:1–10; Jeremiah 23:5) or about the fact that the Messiah
would be born to a virgin (Isaiah 7:13–14)?

Read Matthew 1:18–25. Jewish law set out what Joseph should do as the humiliated groom-to-be by his promised but pregnant bride. Even in his humiliation, Joseph's loving and forgiving spirit shows. He wanted to protect Mary as much as possible, "unwilling to put her to shame" (v. 19). When an angel of the Lord came to Joseph in a dream, Joseph listened. The words of Isaiah 7:14 must have resonated with Joseph: "Behold, the virgin shall conceive and bear a son, and shall call his name Immanuel." When Joseph awoke, he did just as he had been told to do.

Joseph's character suggests that God chose him to be the earthly father of His Son as carefully as He chose Mary to be His Son's mother. Joseph was faithful and obedient, putting the rhythms of his life aside to be a part of fulfilling God's promise of His Son.

What rhythms of life are you most aware of? How do they affect you?

When have those rhythms been challenged? How difficult was it to face those times?

As you pray, rejoice in the rhythms in life that come from God. Ask God to help you understand when His desires may turn your life rhythms upside-down.

Day 10

The Passage of God's Time

And while they were there, the time came for
her to give birth.—Luke 2:6

One of the great truths in life is that the older a person gets,
the faster time seems to go by. Parents of young children
wonder if their children will ever grow up and become independent, and yet regret the passing of time when that happens. Older adults spend time looking back on their lives
and wonder how the time has passed by so quickly. Our
lives are ruled by time.

Time is important in God's plan as well. His plan is
so precise that He could release the details of Jesus' birth
hundreds of years before it ever happened. That statement
is historically and divinely remarkable. For example, somewhere between 742 and 687 B.C.—around 700 years in
advance—the prophet Micah announced that Jesus' birth
would be in Bethlehem (Micah 5:2). Other prophecies include Jeremiah's foretelling that the coming Messiah would
be from the lineage of David, which was given about 600
years in advance (Jeremiah 23:5), and Isaiah's foretelling that
the birth would come through a virgin (Isaiah 7:13–14),
which was given about 700 years before Jesus' birth.

Read Luke 2:1–7. These verses capture a moment in
history—the census that Caesar Augustus, the ruler of the

Roman Empire, required of everyone who was subject to the Rome. Mary's time to give birth came during that historical period. Also, in these verses is a glimpse of eternity— the birth of God's Son whom He sent to earth to restore us eternally back to Him. This moment in time was like none that had ever occurred before, or that will ever come again.

Jesus' coming was prophesied hundreds of years before His birth, and God used Caesar Augustus' census to ensure that His Son was born in Bethlehem. The gospel writer Luke described this convergence of God's plan with the events of human history: "the time came for her to give birth."

How do you see the passing of time in your life? Positively? Negatively? Why?

God existed before the beginning of the world, and He will always exist. With that in mind, what do you think the passing of time means to Him?

As you pray, thank God for His confirmation through history that He is in charge of things as mundane as a census and as incomparable as bringing His Son to us as a part of His plan and in His timing.

Day 11

Angels' Voices

> And suddenly there was with the angel a multitude of the heavenly host praising God and saying, "Glory to God in the highest, and on earth peace among those with whom he is pleased!"—Luke 2:13–14

Is there anything more inspiring than hearing hundreds of musicians sing "The Hallelujah Chorus" from Handel's *Messiah*? Or the sweet pure voices of a children's choir as they sing about Jesus? Or that soloist who has the voice of an angel proclaiming, "How Great Thou Art"? Those voices take us beyond the music itself and into the very presence of God.

Angels are usually seen in the New Testament as messengers. An angel told Zechariah that he would be the father of one who would prepare the way for the Messiah (Luke 1:11–23). The archangel Gabriel angel told Mary that she was the chosen one to be the mother of God's Son (Luke 1:26–38). In three dreams, angels told Joseph that he would be the earthly father of God's Son, and later gave him instructions about the child's welfare (Matthew 1:18–20, 2:12–13, 19–21). God sent His angels to prepare these individuals for what was to come.

Read Luke 2:8–14. Once again, God called on an angel to deliver His message. But this angel's visit was significantly different. The angel didn't come to one of the primary participants in God's story, but appeared in an open field before a group of shepherds. Shepherds were seen as low-class citizens who spent most of their time in the field with their sheep. Their duties did not allow them to keep all the laws and traditions of the rabbis, so they were religious outcasts. No one in Israel would have anticipated that God's angel would be sent to the shepherds. And yet, not only did God send an angel, He showed up Himself. That's what "the glory of the Lord" means. God was there so the shepherds could actually see His presence. To top off this extraordinary experience, a host of angels appeared praising God. How many angels are in a host? The Greek word (*stratia*) means heavenly bodies. Some scholars suggest this means an army of angels, and others suggest that the angel army equaled the stars in the night sky.

Imagine being with the shepherds in the fields at that moment. What might they have felt and experienced?

This message was not just for the shepherds, but for the world—Jesus Christ is God's Son who came to earth for us. How has that message impacted your life?

As you pray, add your voice of praise to the angels' voices, praising aloud, "Glory to God in the highest!"

Day 12

Acts of Worship

> But Mary treasured up all these things, pondering in her heart. And the shepherds returned, glorifying and praising God for all they had heard and seen, as it had been told them.—Luke 2:19–20

The gospel writer Luke never met Jesus and didn't come to faith until later in life. Yet his writings in Luke and Acts are defining works in the New Testament. His gospel account pulls from the gospel of Mark, which was written first, but his account of the movement of God in the early church is totally unique to the New Testament. But how did Luke know things to include that other writers didn't? There are significant details in Luke's gospel found nowhere else. Some scholars believe that Luke was able to interview Mary later in her life to get her eyewitness account of all that happened.

Read Luke 2:15–20. After the angel army departed, the shepherds were left standing in a dark field that had been shining with the light of God's glory and filled with the sounds of praise for the angelic chorus. However, they did not stand around discussing what they had seen. Instead, they left immediately to see the newborn babe. They found the baby and worshipped Him. When they left, they went out into Bethlehem, telling everyone they met about the birth of the Christ Child. Remember they were the ones who been considered to be too unclean to worship at the temple, and yet they were the ones who were given that message to deliver. Their joy was so overwhelming they could not keep it to themselves.

Mary responded differently, possibly because she had spent months carrying the unborn child and reflecting on what she had been chosen to do. With details that could only have come from Mary, Luke explained that Mary added these experiences to those she'd already accumulated and she treasured them. The term *treasured up* is based on a Greek word that can be translated as "to cause oneself to be fully aware of." The term suggests that Mary reflected intently over all she had seen and heard. Today, we would say she thought long and hard about the experiences.

How do you respond to good news in your own life? What would be a reason for holding on to that good news for a while?

The shepherds joyfully and outwardly reflected on the news of Jesus' birth; Mary reflected inwardly, treasuring those moments. Do you respond to God's news like the shepherds or more like Mary?

As you pray, thank God for the joy that the birth of His Son gives to you. Ask Him to teach you how to respond in ways that bring Him glory.

Day 13

Bringing Light to the World

> And going into the house, they saw the child
> with Mary his mother, and they fell down and
> worshiped him.—Matthew 2:11a

Every nativity scene has two stark contrasts, and both are created through the presence of the Magi—the Wise Men. The first contrast is found in the people who are present around the baby. As residents of Nazareth, a small and very poor town, Mary and Joseph would have been poor. They would have been accepted at the temple because of their righteous obedience to the Jewish laws. The shepherds were even poorer than Mary and Joseph and were seen as outcasts. Because of their profession, they were ritually unclean so they were not allowed in the temple. They showed up at the birth straight from their duties in the field, so they were probably dirty from camping out and even smelled like sheep. Yet Mary and Joseph and the gathered shepherds shared one thing in common—they were all Jews.

However, the Magi didn't show up at the cave or the stable at all. They arrived sometime between the time Jesus was presented at the temple when He was forty days old (Luke 2:22) and before He turned two (Matthew 2:13–14). They were not Jews, but pagans from a different land, possibly India, Persia, or Babylon. The Magi were dressed in expensive robes and head garments, traveled in a large caravan of camels, and brought expensive gifts. Although we always think of three of them, one bearing each gift, possibly as many as twelve came to see the Christ Child.

Read Matthew 2:9–12. Following a unique star, the Magi arrived in Jerusalem. Herod summoned them to discover whom they were seeking. When they left Herod, the star they had followed from the east appeared again and led them to the house where Jesus was. There, they worshipped the child and presented expensive gifts to Him. And when they left, they returned home a different way because the Lord warned them of danger in a dream.

The Magi coming to see the Christ Child demonstrated the truths found in Isaiah 49:6 and 60:1–3: God sent His son for everyone—the poor and the rich, the accepted and the outcast, the Jews and the Gentiles. The presence of the Magi showed the birth of the Christ was meant for the entire world.

Read Isaiah 49:6 and 60:1–3. How is God's coming for the Gentiles described?

Based on your understanding of those who came to worship the Christ Child, to which witness do you most relate? Why?

As you pray, praise God for the light that He has brought into your life, and for the darkness that can no longer exist there.

Jesus the Boy

Day 14

Prophetic Bookends

And coming up at that very hour she began to give thanks to God and to speak of him to all who were waiting for the redemption of Jerusalem.—Luke 2:38

Sometimes, God uses "bookend" events to make sure people don't miss what's going on. That's what happened when Mary and Joseph took Jesus to the temple when He was forty days old. The trip from Bethlehem to Jerusalem wasn't very far—about six miles. And with their donkey, the family would have made the trip in two hours, taken care of their duties at the temple, and been home before dark. It should have been a routine trip to the temple—except it wasn't.

Read Luke 2:25–38. Jewish law required that Mary go through purification rites after giving birth, and the parents wanted to present the baby, as their firstborn son, to the Lord. Thousands and thousands of parents had made this same journey to bring their own first sons to God. What took this routine visit from ordinary to extraordinary was the presence of two people who were waiting to see the Christ Child. Simeon is described as a prophet who had been told he would not die until he had met the Christ Child. Anna is described as a prophetess who had spent years at the temple, day and night fasting and in prayer, waiting for the Christ Child. These two are bookends, who by their presence and their understanding anoint this moment in time. In verses 29–32, Simeon rejoiced in prayer, stating that he could now die because he had seen God's prophetic word to him be fulfilled. After his pronouncement, Simeon's work was done. Anna, too, had been waiting for this moment, but her role as witness was just beginning. She began to tell everyone about the child who would bring about the redemption of Jerusalem.

While John the Baptist was given the role of preparing the people for the coming of the Messiah, Simeon was given the role of acknowledging that the Messiah had arrived. Simeon's message ties the prophecy of the Old Testament with the events of the New Testament and brings attention to this pivotal time when God brought His Son into the world to lead us back to Him. Anna picked up the message and shared it with the people. Bookends.

Has God ever "bookended" something in your life to make sure you didn't miss what He was doing? Would you have seen what God was doing without the "bookends"? Why?

In what ways have you shared the work God has done in your life with others?

As you pray, reflect on the people that God has used in your life. Thank God for providing people to you who can speak for Him.

Day 15

To Egypt and Back

> Now when they had departed, behold, an angel of the Lord appeared to Joseph in a dream and said, "Rise, take the child and his mother, and flee to Egypt, and remain there until I tell you, for Herod is about to search for the child, to destroy him."—Matthew 2:13

The story of Joseph taking his family to Egypt and back seems like a sidebar to the story of Jesus' birth. Only Matthew recorded it. Luke didn't mention it and wrote that the family left Bethlehem to return to Galilee. Why the difference? Matthew wrote his gospel for the Jews, carefully recording the prophecies that surrounded Jesus' birth. Luke was writing for Gentiles, so the recording of every prophecy wouldn't have mattered to his audience.

Read Matthew 2:13–23. Matthew wrote that, after the Magi departed, an angel visited Joseph in a dream. The angel told him to take his family to Egypt to keep his family safe from Herod. This was the third time an angel had delivered a message to Joseph. There's no evidence that Joseph ever ignored one of the messages that God sent him, even when the messages were delivered through dreams. The message began with "Rise" or "Get up!" There must have been a sense of urgency in the delivery because Joseph did just that. He got up, packed, and left with the family during the night. They began the long journey to Egypt, one that would have taken almost two weeks and would have had some dangers. But Joseph didn't hesitate in doubt or indecision. The angel instructed Joseph to keep his family in Egypt and to "remain there until I tell you" (v. 13).

Probably Joseph and his family remained in Egypt only a few months before Herod died. Despite the short time frame, the stay in Egypt fulfilled the prophecy of Hosea 11:1: "When Israel was a child, I loved him, and out of Egypt I called my son." Joseph remained obedient and waited for the fourth visit of an angel in a dream to tell him it was safe to return to Israel. Once again, Joseph responded without hesitation and did as he was told. This time, the family returned to Nazareth, responding to a fifth message in a dream that warned Joseph not to settle near Jerusalem.

Do you think Joseph ever got used to these messages coming through dreams? Why?

In what ways does God speak to you?

As you pray, praise God for the fact that He chooses to communicate with you. Ask Him to help you be more attentive to His messages for you.

Day 16

Faith in the Family

> Now his parents went to Jerusalem every year
> at the Feast of the Passover.—Luke 2:41

People for centuries have wondered about Jesus' childhood. Stories abound in apocryphal literature, which has questionable authenticity at best and was never accepted into the canon of scripture. The stories, however, have been widely circulated as true and can be entertaining. For example, one story tells of Jesus putting a dried fish into a basin of water and commanding it to get rid of the salt on its scales and come back to life. According to the story, the fish obeyed.[1] However, the stories take our attention from what Jesus' life and purpose was. Instead, consider what the Bible does show about Jesus' home life.

Read Luke 2:41–42. These two verses give us a glimpse of what Jesus' childhood was like. Jesus was raised in Nazareth, a small town that was located off a major north-south trade route (Matthew 4:15). Life in the town was centered on the Jewish faith. A Jewish man in Jerusalem once explained, "We don't stop to have prayer; we see our whole lives as a prayer, a conversation with God." The men of the

---

[1] Paul L. Maier, *In the Fullness of Time: A Historian Looks at Christmas, Easter, and the Early Church* (Grand Rapids: Kregel Publications, 1991), p. 88.

family daily wore the small tallit, like a vest, under their clothes. Boys as young as three were raised wearing the garment. At the time of becoming a man at thirteen, the young boy added the large tallit or prayer shawl. These were constant reminders of their faith in and relationship to God. The family participated in the local synagogue, and Jesus attended the synagogue school from the age of five, being taught to memorize scripture and read Hebrew.

These things were all prescribed by the laws of their faith and were assumed in verse 41 when the family made their annual trip to Jerusalem to celebrate the Passover. Nazareth was located about ninety miles from Jerusalem, and took five days of walking to get there. The family traveled with friends and other family members on the journey, and along the way, especially as they climbed up the mountain to Jerusalem, they sang the Songs of Ascent from the Psalms. The family demonstrated their righteousness in God in everything they did.

How does this picture of Jesus' family life affirm why Joseph and Mary were chosen to be Jesus' earthly parents?

How do your faith traditions guide your children and family members in faith?

As you pray, ask God to help you be righteous in your daily walk and in daily decisions.

Day 17

Wise in Spirit

And when the feast was ended, as they were returning, the boy Jesus stayed behind in Jerusalem. His parents did not know it.—Luke 2:43

Much of what is known about Jesus' childhood is found in Luke 2:40: "And the child grew and became strong, filled with wisdom. And the favor of God was upon him." In *The Message* Eugene Peterson wrote, "There [Nazareth] the child grew strong in body and was wise in spirit." Jesus grew in the ways that all children grow. His body matured and He developed physical strength. But He also developed in the Lord. Luke didn't share any details of what that meant. However, there are several clues in Luke 2:43–44.

As a parent, I've always wondered how in the world could Mary and Joseph not know where their son was. In our world, it's become unthinkable to let a child, even a twelve-year-old, get out of sight in a busy place. And Jerusalem was packed with people at the time. Historical estimates suggest 250,000 families had crowded inside the city walls for Passover, and each had brought a sheep with them to be sacrificed. The families were required to be in the city seven days before Passover, so they would have crowded in the homes of family members or camped out within the city walls.[1] It was exactly the kind of event that would make modern-day mothers anxious about their children's safety.

Yet Jesus somehow left the family as they were starting their journey home. Maybe both parents assumed that Jesus was with the other one, or with another family member, and they didn't look for Him as they left. Regardless of how it happened, Jesus went out from the family group. He had been in Jerusalem for several days, and this was not His first trip there. He felt comfortable in getting up to the temple. It seems that the Spirit within Him drew Him there. Mary and Joseph had brought Him up to be self-reliant and independent. If Jesus had not been those things, they probably wouldn't have let Him out of their sight.

In what ways would it have been apparent to Mary and Joseph that Jesus' development was unique?

What signs might they have seen that Jesus was "wise in spirit"?

As you pray, ask God to help you be "wise in spirit" as you continue to mature and grow in Him.

---

[1] Paula Fredriksen, "When Jesus Celebrated Passover," *Wall Street Journal*, April 19, 2019; available at https://www.wsj.com/articles/when-jesus-celebrated-passover-11555685683 (subscription required).

Day 18

Searching in Unexpected Places

After three days they found him in the temple.—Luke 2:46a

By the time Mary and Joseph made it to the temple mount seeking their son, two days had passed. That means that after traveling for an entire day without their son, they started the next morning on the one-day trip back to Jerusalem. The fact that it took a day to find Jesus tells us something. Mary and Joseph didn't start looking for Jesus on the temple mount. They spent a day looking for Him everywhere else in Jerusalem. Luke didn't give any details, except the passage of time. Imagine where parents would seek a missing twelve-year-old today—at a friend's house playing video games, or off on his bicycle, or skateboarding at a park. Even in first-century Jerusalem, there were places that Mary and Joseph expected Jesus to be. Apparently, they were wrong, and according to the old adage, they found Him in the last place they expected Him to be.

Read Luke 2:45–46. Joseph and Mary must have felt anxious at His absence and urgency in the need to locate Him. It wasn't until they eliminated all other possibilities that they looked for Him in the temple complex. Can you imagine their surprise when they found Jesus, this boy who was not yet seen as a man, sitting at the temple with the rabbis?

Mary and Joseph had a difficult assignment as Jesus' earthly parents. They knew who Jesus was and they knew what He had come to do. That knowledge had to be in their minds at all times. Yet, there had to be moments—like finding Jesus in the temple—when what they knew about Him became clearly seen in what He chose to do.

What feelings and thoughts would Mary and Joseph have struggled with while they searched for Jesus? How would their knowledge of who Jesus was have impacted those feelings?

Why would the temple have been an unexpected place for Jesus to be? What do you think Mary and Joseph felt when they found Jesus in the temple? How would this have clarified their understanding of their role as Jesus' earthly parents?

As you pray, ask God to help you see Him in the unexpected places as well as the expected places in your life.

$\mathcal{Day}\ 19$

Astonishing the Teachers

And all who heard him were amazed at his understanding and his answers.—Luke 2:47

According to scripture, Jesus' hometown of Nazareth was
given a bad reputation. When Philip told of having met the
Messiah from Nazareth, Nathanael asked, "Can anything
good come out of Nazareth?" (John 1:43–46) The people
of Galilee in the first century have been described as faithful. They lived near a major trade route so they interacted
with people of the world and were multilingual. They were
highly educated in the scripture of the Old Testament and
righteously followed the laws prescribed there. Within their
synagogues, deep discussion on scripture would have tak-
en place regularly. They memorized scripture and lived according to the Shema (Deut. 6:5). The best and brightest
of these students were able to continue their studies into
adulthood as they learned a trade to earn their livelihood.
This school was the Beth Midrash, in which they learned
how to intently study and interpret the Torah.[1]

This is the community in which God had chosen for
His Son to be raised. And this background probably helped
explain the events that took place in Jerusalem when Jesus
went missing. Read Luke 2:46b–48. Jesus was not of an age to

---

[1] Adapted from "Rabbi and Talmidim," at https://www.thatthe-
worldmayknow.com/rabbi-and-talmidim.

have entered the Beth Midrash school yet, but He was found at the feet of the rabbis, not just listening to their teachings but participating with questions of His own and giving deep, well-thought-out answers. Even the rabbis were "astounded at His understanding and His answers." It has been suggested in commentaries that Jesus' answers were not the boyish questions one would expect from a twelve-year-old, but were "the kind of probing questions used in ancient academics and similar discussions." One biblical scholar wrote that Jesus participated in a Midrashic discussion of the Bible in such depth that "their amazement must relate to his deducting things from Scripture which they had never found before."[2]

It's no wonder that the rabbis and the other students were astonished at what they heard. Some of Jesus' questions had never been considered before by the rabbis, and yet their response suggests that those questions should have been.

What does it mean to you to think deeply about God's Word?

How do you think Jesus was able to think so deeply about God's Word that it was a surprise to all who saw it?

As you pray, ask God to give you a desire to keep digging deeper into His Word and being astonished by it as you study.

---

[2] Frank E. Gaebelein, gen. ed., *Expositor's Bible Commentary: Matthew, Mark, Luke*, vol. 8 (Grand Rapids, MI: Zondervan, 1984), p. 852.

Day 20

At His Father's Business

And he said to them, "Why were you looking for me? Did you not know that I must be in my Father's house?"—Luke 2:49

Herod's Great Temple covered the entire temple mount, and its size is difficult to comprehend. The eastern and western walls each measured 1,590 feet in length (about the length of four and a half football fields). Inside the walls, the area was divided into the court of the Gentiles, and the areas of the temple itself. Inside the walled area of the temple was the court of the women. The women's court was also used by men and children, but it was the only place women were allowed to go. Through a gate was another courtyard, referred to as the court of the men or the court of Israel, where only the men and priests could go. The part of the temple that housed the Holy of Holies was sixty feet high.[1] The temple area also had many entrances onto the temple mount. The court of the Gentiles was open to all, so it was filled with market stalls and people hawking their wares. It is hard to get a sense of size just from the dimensions, but imagine how overwhelming it would have been to come

---

[1] Justin Taylor, "What Did the Temple Look Like in Jesus' Time?"; available at https://www.thegospelcoalition.org/blogs/justin-taylor/what-did-the-temple-look-like-in-jesus-time/.

into the temple area looking for a missing child. The rabbis could have been teaching in the outer court of the Gentiles, in the court of women, or even in the court of the men.

Read Luke 2:49–52. After searching for a day throughout Jerusalem, Jesus' parents finally located Him at the temple. The statement, "They were astonished," seems to be an understatement. They must have been emotionally and physically drained. It's no wonder that Mary asked Him why He had mistreated them by disappearing. "Searching in great distress" seems like an understatement too. They must have been panicked. Yet Jesus' response didn't speak to their fears or their feelings. He questioned why they had even looked for Him because they should have known that He would be in His Father's house. *The Message* says that Jesus was there dealing with the things of His Father.

How do you think Jesus came to understand that He had something special to do for His Father?

Since Mary and Joseph knew of Jesus' identity from before His birth, do you think they were surprised by what He said and what He had done? Why?

As you pray, thank God for what He has done in your life. Ask God to let you know how He can use you in a new way.

Jesus the Man

Key Passage
Philippians 2:7

Day 21

Jesus Became Flesh

And the Word became flesh and dwelt among us, and we have seen his glory, glory as of the only Son from the Father, full of grace and truth.—John 1:14

The early church struggled under the teaching of Gnosticism. Gnosticism was a series of false teachings that attacked who Jesus was. One falsehood was the belief that the physical body in itself was corrupt and was the source of evil. If this belief was accepted, the next logical step was that since Jesus was pure and without sin, He couldn't have taken on a physical body—He couldn't have been human. Take that idea a step further, and His work on the cross to bring salvation was denied. Some false teachers went so far as to deny Jesus' birth to Mary, and suggested that Jesus only came to earth to inhabit a human body just in time to lead in ministry. It's easy to see how dangerous this view was to the foundational understanding of Jesus in the early church. John addressed Jesus' humanity as he wrote the first chapter of his gospel.

Read John 1:1–5, 14–16. God's plan was to bring life to humanity through His Son Jesus Christ. Jesus became human. He took the form of flesh and bone. John did not elaborate on the details of the Word becoming flesh, but the Gospels of Matthew and Luke provide the story of Jesus' miraculous conception and birth to a virgin. Jesus took on human flesh and came to earth to "make His dwelling" among us. The phrase "make His dwelling" is the same used for "pitched His tent" or "tabernacle." Jesus came as God's physical dwelling on earth. He did not cease to be God. Of course, He had certain limitations because of His humanity.

Jesus was more than a symbol. He was the visible, human expression of God's presence. Jesus was as much God as He was human. He was fully God and fully man.

Why do you think false teachings about Jesus became an issue to the early church? Why would people have felt the need to deny Jesus' humanity and focus only on His divinity?

Why does it matter to you that Jesus was totally human?

Read John 3:16 as a prayer and thank God for His willingness to send His only Son to bring you salvation. Ask God to show you opportunities to share that verse during this period of Advent.

Day 22

Survival Needs

> Then Jesus was led up by the Spirit into the
> wilderness to be tempted by the devil. And af-
> ter fasting forty days and forty nights, he was
> hungry.—Matthew 4:1–2

Jesus' temptation in the wilderness near the Dead Sea is fully recorded in two of the synoptic gospels—Matthew and
Luke. Both state Jesus was tempted by the devil for forty
days. The Greek word used for the temptations indicates
that they were continuous—they kept coming in an ongo-
ing barrage. Throughout history, some have claimed that if
Jesus were God in the flesh, He could not have sinned by
giving in to temptation. Such statements deny His humanity. Jesus was fully God and fully human. In becoming a man,
God subjected Himself to the trials of humanity, which are
otherwise incompatible with His deity (Philippians 2:5–
11). We know, for example, it is impossible for the Eternal
God to die. However, Christ not only could die, He actually
did. We might ask whether God can be in need of anything.
God is completely sufficient in Himself. Yet in Jesus, God
placed Himself in need of human requirements for life—
food, water, clothing, and shelter.

Read Matthew 4:1–4. After Jesus' baptism, He was
led by the Holy Spirit to an arid wasteland to be tested.

According to James 1:13, good cannot be tempted by evil. But Jesus, both fully human and fully divine, could be tempted just as the rest of humanity can be. For forty days, Jesus did not eat. Imagine the impact on the body for not eating for forty days. Physical weakness and exhaustion had set in, leaving Jesus vulnerable. Satan tried to take advantage of that vulnerability, encouraging Jesus to feed Himself by using His power to turn rocks into bread. He might have been suggesting that God had not provided for His Son. Or he may have been trying to convince Jesus that He would be unable to do what God had called Him to do if He died from starvation.

Jesus could have bailed at any moment. But He did not. He did not settle for a quick end to His ordeal, but instead, He trusted God, using the words from scripture to defend the attack.

Put yourself in Jesus' place in the wilderness. After forty days, how would you have felt mentally, emotionally, physically, and spiritually?

In what ways does Jesus' ability to withstand temptation provide hope for you when you face temptation?

As you pray, acknowledge how Jesus suffered for you. Ask God to help you stand firm when you face temptations.

Day 23

Ministering Angels

Then the devil left him, and behold, angels came
and were ministering to him.—Matthew 4:11

While Matthew and Luke both included complete records
on Jesus' temptation, Mark only gave it three sentences in
English. His account was written first, and it includes an
interesting statement: "And the angels began to serve Him"
(Mark 1:13). Matthew had Mark's gospel available to him
when he wrote his account of Jesus' temptations, and he
included that fact as well. In both Matthew and Mark, the
temptation account ends with the angels. We've already
seen angels present at each important event in Jesus' life, beginning with the angel who told Zechariah that he and his
wife Elizabeth would be parents of the one who would prepare the way for the Messiah. Up to this point in Jesus' story,
the angels had been there to deliver God's messages. But in
the wilderness, the angels came to serve Jesus physically.

Read Matthew 4:5–11. In the second temptation, Satan
challenged Jesus to throw Himself off the high pinnacle of
the temple so the angels would stop His fall and save Him.
Satan's goal was to get Jesus to test God. Jesus rejected the
challenge, just as He had the challenge of feeding Himself.
Satan took Jesus then to a high mountain and challenged
Jesus again to use His power. This time, Satan's desire was
to get Jesus to worship him instead of God. Again, Jesus

rejected Satan, and Satan finally left. Physically, Jesus needed help after fasting and experiencing these encounters with Satan. So God had His ministering angels feed Jesus and take care of Him spiritually. In verse 6, Satan had encouraged Jesus to get help from the angels. But only when this battle of wills between Jesus and Satan was over did the angels come. They came on God's timetable, not Satan's.

Nineteenth-century preacher Charles Spurgeon described this encounter between the angels and Jesus: "They must have been amazed when they saw Him born on earth and living here in poverty! And when they saw Him tempted of the enemy, they must have loathed the adversary. How could Satan be permitted to come so near their pure and holy Master?"[1] When Jesus was at His weakest, the angels took care of His needs.

If the angels had shown up before Jesus' battle with Satan was complete, how could their presence have impacted the outcome?

How do the angels ministering to Jesus give evidence of His humanity?

As you pray, thank the Lord for the evidence that shows how He allowed His Son to face life's struggles as you have faced them.

---

[1] Charles Spurgeon, "Satan Departing, Angels Ministering," Sermon #2326; available at https://www.spurgeongems.org/vols37-39/chs2326.pdf.

Day 24

Astounded by Belief

When Jesus heard this, he marveled and
said to those who followed him, "Truly, I tell
you, with no one in Israel have I found such
faith."—Matthew 8:10

One of the characteristics of God is that He is omniscient or
all-knowing. Theologian A. W. Tozer describes God's omni-
science this way: "To say that God is omniscient is to say that
He possesses perfect knowledge and therefore has no need
to learn. But it is more: It is to say that God has never learned
and cannot learn."[1] That means that God has always known
everything—there is nothing for Him to learn. Therefore, the
Son of God has all knowledge as well. There is nothing He
could learn. How, then, could Jesus have been surprised by
someone? The fact that He could points to the human nature
that He took on. In His humanity, Jesus could be surprised.

Read Matthew 8:5–13. The centurion was a leader of one
hundred men in the Roman army. He understood military life,
especially the chain of command and following orders. This
centurion was a Gentile and had no knowledge of the Old
Testament promises of the Messiah to come. In fact, he would
not have understood, much less believed, the idea of One
all-knowing, all-powerful God. Yet somehow this centurion

---

[1] A. W. Tozer, *The Knowledge of the Holy: The Attributes of God* (New
York: Harper Collins, 1961), p. 55.

had seen through Jesus' humanity and recognized the divine power within Him. The centurion understood that if Jesus commanded something to happen, whatever it was, it would take place. And Jesus marveled or was astonished at the centurion's faith. *Expositor's Commentary* states that "amazement is not appropriate for God, seeing it must arise from new and unexpected happenings, yet it could occur in Christ, inasmuch as he had taken on our human emotions, along with our flesh."[2] As a man, Jesus could be surprised or astonished—He could learn from the unexpected. What surprised Jesus was the level of the centurion's faith—he had "penetrated more deeply the nature of Jesus' person and authority than any Jew of his time."[3]

Reflect on all the Old Testament prophecies that pointed directly to the coming of Jesus. Why do you think the centurion was able to see Jesus' identity as Messiah while those who had studied the prophecies could not?

Describe the evidence of Jesus' humanity uncovered so far in this study. What does this evidence suggest?

As you pray, acknowledge Jesus' humanity. Ask God to help you see Him more clearly through Jesus' humanity.

---

[2] Frank E. Gaebelein, gen. ed., *The Expositor's Bible Commentary: Matthew, Mark, Luke*, vol. 8 (Grand Rapids: Zondervan Publishing, 1984), p. 202.

[3] Gaebelein, p. 202.

Day 25

What Jesus Looked Like

Jacob's well was there; so Jesus, wearied as he was from his journey, was sitting beside the well.—John 4:6

Very little is given in the Bible about what Jesus physically looked like. While both Moses and David were described as "handsome," Jesus' only description is found in Isaiah—"He had no form or majesty that we should look at him, and no beauty that we should desire him" (v. 2). Through her research, Joan Taylor has provided some physical details for us. Jesus was of average height for the period, probably about 5'5". From archaeological and historical evidence, she has concluded that His eyes and hair were dark, and probably couldn't have been distinguished from the Egyptians of the time. Because He walked so much and ate sparingly, He was probably thin, but He would have been in good physical condition because of His carpentry work. She wrote, "Jesus was a man who was physical in terms of the labor that he came from."[1]

Read John 4:1–6. In chapter 3, John's disciples questioned why Jesus was drawing so many people to Him, and in John 4:1, the Pharisees noticed Jesus' new converts. Not

---

[1] Owen Jarus, "What Did Jesus Really Look Like? New Study Redraws Holy Image," *Live Science Contributor*, February 27, 2018.

wanting attention, Jesus left Judea from somewhere around Jerusalem, and headed to Galilee. The distance would have been around one hundred miles, and would have taken five days or so of walking. Most Jews would have crossed the Jordan River toward the east as the journey began so they would miss having to go through Samaria. Jesus, however, intentionally went through Samaria, probably for a divine appointment with the woman at the well. Even in this divine appointment, Jesus' humanity is apparent. He was tired from the long walk. He was thirsty from the heat of the journey. He needed to sit down and rest. Even in His strong physical condition, Jesus was subject to the same frailties that we are—He could run out of energy, He needed rest, and He needed food and drink.

Jesus knew where God wanted Him to go and He obeyed completely. But, despite His divinity, His physical body had limits—even one in excellent physical condition still needed to be kept refreshed and rested.

Why do you think scripture provides no real description of what Jesus looked like? Would knowing what He looked like impact how you view Him? Why?

Do you think Jesus' human limitations hindered His ministry or helped it? Why?

As you pray, thank God for allowing Jesus to be totally human in all ways, even in the ways that limited Him physically.

Day 26

Tears of Grief

When Jesus saw her weeping, and the Jews who had come with her also weeping, he was deeply moved in his spirit and greatly troubled.—John 11:33

Possibly one of the most frequent questions for students of the Bible is why did Jesus weep for Lazarus when He knew He could bring Lazarus back from the grave. It's a fair question. Jesus had received word that His friend Lazarus was very ill, and instead of rushing to Lazarus's side, Jesus stayed where He was for two more days. Not only that, but Jesus loved Lazarus's sisters, Mary and Martha, as well. Jesus had to have known how much they needed Him. Yet, by the time Jesus arrived, Lazarus had already passed away (John 11:5–7). Imagine the chaos when Jesus arrived. Lazarus had already been in the tomb four days, and many of the family's friends had come to grieve with them.

Read John 11:20–35. When Martha heard Jesus had finally come, she went outside and confronted Him about His delay. Martha even told Jesus that if He had come on time, her brother would have lived. And in total faith, she asked Jesus to restore her brother. Jesus answered her calmly and talked to her about faith. But when Mary arrived, she fell at Jesus' feet, weeping in sorrow and lamenting that He had come too late. So why did Jesus weep then?

Some scholars point to this event as one of those times when Jesus' humanity and divinity can be clearly seen working together. Jesus identified with Mary's distress and was "deeply moved"—from a Greek word that means angry—and "greatly troubled"—from a Greek word that means agitated.[1] Obviously, Jesus wasn't angry with the sisters or with Lazarus. These words suggest that Jesus was angry with being confronted by the permanence of death that can come in the world through sin.[2]

Jesus felt the crisis of death and grief, and in that moment, He wept with Mary. Williams's biblical translation states this as, "Jesus burst into tears."[3] Even those who witnessed Jesus' tears were surprised by the depth of His emotion.

> How do you see Jesus' humanity in these verses?
>
> How do you see His divinity portrayed? Was His divinity ever at odds with His humanity? Why?
>
> As you pray, acknowledge the human emotions that you're dealing with and ask God to teach you how to see Jesus' compassion even when deeply troubled.

---

[1] Frank E. Gaebelein, gen. ed., *The Expositor's Bible Commentary: John and Acts*, vol. 9 (Grand Rapids: Zondervan Publishing, 1981), p. 119.

[2] Gaebelein, p. 119.

[3] Gaebelein, p. 119.

Day 27

Not My Will

For I have come down from heaven, not to
do my own will but the will of him who sent
me.—John 6:38

As individuals, we each have a distinct will. That *will* guides
our decisions, our desires, and our choices in life, and its
presence makes us uniquely human. When Jesus came to
earth to be human like us, He too had a human will. Part
of the perfect duality in Christ—that He was totally divine
and totally human—was demonstrated in the presence of
His divine will and His human will.

Jesus acknowledged His human will twice in scriptur-
al accounts—once while preaching on the shore of Galilee
and once while praying in the Garden of Gethsemane the
night He was arrested. Both times, Jesus mentioned His
own will in conjunction with the will of His Father.

Read John 6:35–40. People who had heard Jesus teach
on the mountainside and had eaten from the miraculous
food Jesus provided came looking for Jesus. They wanted
more. They wanted to know what they needed to do for
eternal life. Jesus told them that He was the bread of life who
had come to do His Father's will, not His own.

In the Garden of Gethsemane, Jesus asked if it was possible
for Him not to have to die on the cross (Matthew 26:39). The
important word in that statement is "*if.*" Jesus asked only if it

was possible, but never argued against the will of His Father. The Son of God came to do the will of the Father. This battle of wills, of the human desire to avoid the pain and of the divine desire to submit to the will of His Father, was very real at Gethsemane. In fact, it was the victory of the human will submitting completely to the Father's will that made Jesus' sacrificial death on the cross possible. Romans 5:19 states, "For as by the one man's disobedience the many were made sinners, so by the one man's obedience the many will be made righteous." That could only have happened through Jesus' submission of His human will. David Mathis wrote that Jesus had "a fine human will that, while being an authentic human will, is perfectly in sync with, and submissive to, the divine will."[1]

How difficult do you think it was for Jesus to submit His human will to the Father? Read Matthew 26:36–44. Does your impression support the evidence from the Garden? Why?

How can believers submit their wills to the Father's?

As you pray, ask God to help you be in sync with His will in your life.

---

[1] David Mathis, "Jesus Is Fully Heaven," www.desiringGod.com, December 15, 2016.

Jesus the Messiah

Key Passage
Mark 1:11

Day 28

The Presence of the Trinity

And a voice came from heaven, "You are My
beloved Son; with you I am well pleased!"
—Mark 1:11

Jesus' baptism was a significant moment in His life. It stands
as the moment when John the Baptist passed the torch on to
Jesus. It's the moment of Jesus' anointing before He began
His ministry on earth, and His commissioning to carry out
that ministry. It was so significant that all three of the synoptic
gospel writers included it in their accounts. Matthew included
John's reluctance to baptize Jesus in a total of five verses. Luke
used only two verses. Mark gave it fifty-three words in Greek, or
three short sentences in English. Luke and Mark quoted God's
words for Jesus as, "You are My beloved Son; I take delight in
You!" Since we typically look at the longer version for Matthew,
we sometimes miss the great truths in Mark's account.

Read Mark 1:9–11. After Jesus came up from the water, three divine things occurred. First, Jesus watched as
the heavens were torn open above Him. That moment was
something Isaiah 64:1 had prophesized. Mark used the
Greek word *schizein* twice in his gospel, here and when the
temple veil was torn (15:38). The word carries the idea of
a cataclysmic event—something only God could do. Both
times Mark used it to reveal Jesus as the Son of God. Second, Jesus watched the Holy Spirit descend like a dove.

Some scholars see this moment as the Holy Spirit returning to Israel since He departed the temple in Jerusalem (Ezekiel 10).[1] Third, Jesus heard the voice of His Father whose words were spoken directly to Him. Matthew recorded God's words as, "This is My beloved Son." Some scholars suggest that God spoke twice, once directly to His Son and then a second time to the witnesses, acknowledging His Son.

One of the interesting things about Jesus' baptism is that the entire Trinity—Father, Son, and Holy Spirit—were present in this event. And all Three were doing different things, showing how the Trinity not only exists in Three but works in Three as well.

Carefully look at the work of each member in the Trinity in this passage. How do you see their work as a reflection of their role in the Trinity?

How would you explain the significance of the Three being together in this event?

As you pray, acknowledge the presence of the Father, the Son, and the Holy Spirit in your life and ask for a clearer understanding of the Three in your life.

---

[1] James R. Edwards, The Baptism of Jesus According to the Gospel of Mark," JETS 34/1 (March 1991): 43-57; available at https://www.etsjets.org/files/JETS-PDFs/34/34-1/34-1-pp043-057_JETS.pdf.

Day 29

Revealed to His Disciples

This, the first of his signs, Jesus did at Cana in
Galilee, and manifested His glory. And his disciples believed in him.—John 2:11

The only gospel to include an account of Jesus' miracle in
Cana was John. Why? Because John was one of the first disciples Jesus recruited. Because John attended the wedding
in Cana. Because John saw it all happen firsthand.

Read John 2:1–11. Jesus attended a family wedding with
five or six of His disciples. The wedding was not long after
Jesus' temptations, maybe a month or so, and He was just
at the beginning of His ministry. While at the wedding, the
supply of wine ran out—something that would have been a
humiliation for the family. Jesus' mother, Mary, was also at the
wedding, and she asked her Son to help out the family with
the wine supply. Notice she didn't tell Him how to, she simply trusted that He could. Jesus went from being one of the
guests to revealing His glory before His disciples by changing
the water into wine. He used no words. He never touched the
water or the water jars. He simply willed the wine into being.
And the water responded to His will and became wine.

A couple of things are interesting to note. First, this
was Jesus' first miracle, and He chose to do the miraculous at a small gathering, rather than a large affair or at

the temple. Jesus didn't want the fanfare or attention. He simply responded to a need in compassion. Second, Jesus carefully made sure that people unconnected to Him were involved—He instructed the servants on what to do and He allowed the master of the feast to be the judge. There could be no question that the water had miraculously turned to wine at His will. Third, Jesus chose to reveal Himself to His disciples at this early point in His ministry. Jesus called them to follow Him and they had obeyed. In witnessing this first miracle, His disciples were confronted with the fact that Jesus could do whatever He said He could.

Mary had watched Jesus grow into adulthood and she knew the truth of His birth. Do you think that understanding helped her recognize the possibilities of what Jesus could do? Why?

The disciples had followed Jesus as soon as He called them, and then they saw evidence of His power. Has your growing relationship with Jesus been similar? Why?

As you pray, reflect on the phrase, "manifested his glory." Acknowledge how you see Jesus' glory in your life, and thank God for revealing His Son to the world.

Day 30

The Miracle of Healing

> When Jesus saw him lying there and knew that
> he had already been there a long time, he said
> to him, "Do you want to be healed?"—John 5:6

John's gospel records the majority of Jesus' miracles. He explained why these miracles or signs were so important in John 20:30–31: "Now Jesus did many other signs in the presence of the disciples, which are not written in this book; but these are written so that you may believe that Jesus is the Christ, the Son of God, and that by believing you may have life in his name." Interestingly, more than half of Jesus' miracles were for people who needed help—the diseased and the handicapped.[1] One of the more thought-provoking of these miracles was the healing of the lame man at the pool of Bethseda.

Read John 5:2–9. On His way to Jerusalem, Jesus stopped at the pool of Bethseda. People believed that the waters there were stirred occasionally by angels, and the person who was able to get to the waters first after this stirring would be healed.

The man Jesus approached had been there for most of his life. He was older. He was probably paralyzed. He was

---

[1] Paul L. Maier, *In the Fullness of Time: A Historian Looks at Christmas, Easter, and the Early Church* (Grand Rapids: Kregel Publications, 1991), p. 102.

hopeless. Notice that when Jesus saw the man lying there, He knew the man's life history. He had divine knowledge of the man's condition and His experiences. Jesus knew the man was hopeless, so He asked him, "Do you *really* want to be healed?" Of course the man did, right? But what was required to be healed took tremendous trust and great faith. Jesus told the man who was paralyzed to get up, pick up his bed mat, and go home. The man who had laid there for thirty-eight years because he *couldn't* get up immediately got up in obedience.

Charles Spurgeon sermonized that the man lay there waiting for Jesus to come save him.[2] Have you ever waited on Jesus—looking for a sign, listening for His voice, praying and praying for Him to tell you what to do? How difficult is waiting on the Lord? What have you learned in the process?

What does the fact that half of Jesus' miracles were for people in need suggest about His concern for you?

As you pray, praise God for His Son who cares deeply and personally about what happens to you.

---

[2] Charles Spurgeon, *Impotence and Omnipotence*, Sermon #2269, Feb. 16, 1890; at https://www.spurgeon.org/resource-library/sermons/impotence-and-omnipotence#flipbook/.

Power over Nature

And they were filled with great fear and said to one another, "Who then is this, that even the wind and the sea obey him?"—Mark 4:41

Some of Jesus' miracles were about His power over nature. The first of those, Jesus' miracle of calming the storm at sea, is included in all three of the synoptic gospels: Matthew 8:23–27, Mark 4:35–41, and Luke 8:22–25. The storm came up suddenly on the Sea of Galilee just after Jesus and His disciples had left by boat from the shore where Jesus had been teaching. According to Mark 4:1, Jesus had taught His largest crowd ever for the day, and He was exhausted. Mark's account, the longest of the three, includes some interesting details.

Read Mark 4:35–41. After getting in the boat, Jesus went to the stern and fell deeply asleep. Then, a terrible storm came up. The Sea of Galilee is known for having major storms that come up quickly, but those are most often in the daytime. When a storm arises at night, it's even more horrific. Mark described it as "a furious squall," while Matthew used the Greek word *seismos*, which is used in scripture for an earthquake or a sea storm. Luke described the boat as being swamped with water and in danger of going under. In the midst of this raging squall, Jesus slept soundly. Why? Most scholars suggest that Jesus was exhausted but perfectly at peace in the hands of His Father, knowing that His time to die had not yet come.[1]

Mark quoted Jesus as telling the storm, "Peace! Be still!" Mark, Matthew, and Luke all used the image of an exorcism as Jesus rebuked the winds and the sea. Some scholars believe that this horrific, unusual storm was actually an attack by Satan targeting Jesus and His disciples.[2] This is possibly born out through the reaction of the disciples after Jesus calmed the storm. They were afraid, no longer of the storm, but of the complete power that Jesus held over nature. If scholars are correct that this was a satanic attack, Jesus then also demonstrated His power over Satan as well. No wonder the disciples were overwhelmed by what they had seen.

How do you feel when you are confronted with Jesus' power over all things? Are you overwhelmed, amazed, afraid, or uplifted? Why?

In what ways have you seen the power of Jesus working in your own life?

As you pray, acknowledge the divine power that Jesus has as the Son of God, as the Messiah, and as your Savior. Thank God for allowing Jesus to demonstrate that power before man, before nature, and, especially, before Satan.

---

[1] Frank E. Gaebelein, gen. ed., *The Expositor's Bible Commentary: Matthew, Mark, Luke*, vol. 8 (Grand Rapids: Zondervan, 1984), pp. 215, 655, 911.

[2] Craig Blomberg, *The New American Commentary: Matthew* (Nashville: Broadman & Holman, 1992), p. 149; Herbert Lockyer, *All the Miracles of the Bible* (Grand Rapids: Zondervan, 1961), p. 183.

Day 32

Even the Rocks Praise Him

He answered, "I tell you, if these were silent,
the very stones would cry out."—Luke 19:40

Only Luke recorded the story of Jesus weeping over the city
of Jerusalem. It was a private moment in which Jesus wept for
the city that had rejected Him, for the Jewish leaders who had
refused to accept His identity as Messiah, and for the Jewish
people who had failed to hear His purpose as their Savior. That
emotional moment for Jesus came after His triumphant entry
into Jerusalem and His confrontation with the Pharisees who
asked Him to quiet the crowds who offered Him praises.

Read Luke 19:36–44. Jesus' disciples had begun to
praise their Lord as they moved down the road on the
Mount of Olives, leading Jesus as He rode on a borrowed
donkey. For them, this must have been one of those amazing
moments when everything seemed to finally come together
in Jesus' ministry. Jews heard of Jesus' approach and came
to welcome Him into the city. The Pharisees also heard Jesus was on His way and they became angry at the crowd's
demonstration of their praise for Jesus. The Pharisees asked
Jesus to rebuke His disciples, and to make His disciples stop
praising Him.

In this passage are two pictures of Jesus' divinity. First,
Jesus responded to the Pharisees that if people stopped

praising Him, the very stones would do so. Not only did His response speak to His divine identity as God's Son, it also spoke to His divine identity as Creator. If stones could speak, they too would have joined the disciples in praising Jesus. Their words would have proclaimed His creativity in designing the world and His power over creation. Even today, Israel is full of rocks. Jesus' response creates the picture of the entire created universe bending before the One who created it.

Second, Jesus wept over the city of Jerusalem for its lostness. This was not human concern for the people of the city, but divine anguish over those who would never hear Him, never receive forgiveness, and never be redeemed before God.

Read today's passage again, focusing on the words that describe Jesus' divine identity. How do these words convey Jesus as part of the Trinity?

Look outside your window at God's creation. If creation praised its Creator, what do you think it would say?

As you pray, remember that you are part of God's creation and praise God the Father who sent His only Son to be with us, the Son who came to us so that we could have life in Him, and the Holy Spirit for His presence in your life.

Day 33

Jesus Proclaimed His Messiahship

And I tell you, you are Peter, and on this rock I will build my church, and the gates of hell shall not prevail against it.—Matthew 16:18

In the first century, Caesarea Philippi was a thriving city and cult worship center. The city's name was in honor of Herod's son Philip who ruled over the area, but it was also known by Panias (also written as Banias), its Greek name. Panias was the center of worship for the Greek god Pan, who was part man and part goat. The worship complex included a temple for worship of Pan, pools of water for sacrificial bathing, a temple dwelling for the temple virgins, and a cave where human sacrifices were made. Sexual activity was part of the worship, and participants were free to have sex in an open area of the complex.

Read Matthew 16:13–20. Jesus took His disciples north from Galilee to Caesarea Philippi. It was a pagan city that no good Jew would have been caught dead in. Yet Jesus took them there to a place where they could see as His backdrop the temple complex, the sacrifices to pagan gods, the sexual immorality, and the bottomless cave that had accepted so many living sacrifices. In that place, Jesus asked His disciples who they thought He was. When Peter proclaimed that

Jesus was the Christ—the Messiah and the Son of God, Jesus responded that Peter had been given divine knowledge to know that. In response, Jesus revealed that He was the Messiah and that He would one day build His church that could withstand even the gates of hell.

This is one of those passages best understood when studied in its physical context. The cave that had accepted living sacrifices was known as the Gates of Hell. In that pagan place, full of idolatry, sexual immorality, temple virgins, and live sacrifices, Jesus told His disciples that no evil, even the Gates of Hell, would ever be strong enough to stand against Him—the Messiah, the Christ, the one Living Sacrifice that would never need to be repeated.

Unbelievably, the pagan worship of Pan continued at Caesarea Philippi until the 5th century A.D. But Jesus' revelation to His disciples in that place also revealed that He will one day be victorious in His battle against evil.

How do you see the church today stand against that evil?

The book of Revelation promises that Jesus will return to defeat Satan. What is your role while you wait for that to happen?

As you pray, ask God to help you boldly proclaim Jesus the Messiah to others.

Day 34

Instituting the Lord's Supper

> And he took bread, and when he had given
> thanks, he broke it and gave it to them, saying,
> "This is my body, which is given for you. Do
> this in remembrance of me."—Luke 22:19

J. Vernon McGee wrote, "The Tabernacle is the finest portrait of Christ and of His redemption that there is in the Old Testament. God sent a picture before He sent the Person. The Tabernacle is God's picture book for babes in Christ."[1] Think of the implications of that statement.

Everything in the first tabernacle, which was created exactly as God instructed it to be, pointed to the coming Messiah. For example, the shewbread and the lampstand in the Holy Place represented Jesus as the bread of life and the light of the world. And, in the outer court, the bronze laver or basin in which the priests sacrificially cleansed themselves for their sins represented the cleansing from sin that Christ would provide through the cross.[2] By worshipping at the tabernacle and the temples that followed, God's priests and people looked ahead at the One who would one day bring them eternal redemption.

---

[1] J. Vernon McGee, *The Tabernacle: God's Portrait of Christ* (Pasadena, CA: Thru the Bible Radio Network, 2002), n.p.; available at https://www.ttb.org/docs/default-source/Booklets/tabernacle.pdf?sfvrsn=2.

[2] McGee, p. 57.

Read Luke 22:14–20. The gospels disagree about when this Passover Feast took place. Matthew, Mark, and Luke recorded this as the Passover meal; John recorded this meal as taking place the night before the Passover Feast. Regardless of when the meal took place, Jesus knew that it was His last opportunity to be with His disciples in this way. He knew that His life would be sacrificed at Passover.

During the Passover Feast, Jesus used the elements that had been part of the Jewish tradition since they left Egypt as slaves. For the Jews, each element of the feast was a reminder of God's redemptive work in their past. God had brought them out of Egypt, through the wilderness, and into the Promised Land. Passover was a time of celebration for all God had done in the past. But Jesus used the elements to bring God's redemptive story to the present—to His redemptive work on the cross. Paul Maier described Jesus' Last Supper this way: "Jesus inaugurated what became the longest continuous meal in history, for soon his followers would start celebrating, in which someone, somewhere in the world, has been offering up bread and wine in a similar matter nearly every moment since."[3]

How does your worship in church differ from worship in the tabernacle?

What do these differences show about Jesus Christ?

As you pray, reflect on Hebrews 9:11–12. Acknowledge that Jesus is your Passover Lamb whose death on the cross has paid for your sin.

---

[3] Paul Maier, *In the Fullness of Time: A Historian Looks at Christmas, Easter, and the Early Church* (Grand Rapids, Kregel Publications, 1991), pp. 126, 127.

Jesus the Savior and Redeemer

Key Passage
Matthew 34:20

Day 35

The Radiance of the Glory of God

> He is the radiance of the glory of God and the exact imprint of his nature, and he upholds the universe by the word of his power. After making purification for sins, he sat down at the right hand of the Majesty on high.—Hebrews 1:3

Moses came as close to the presence of God as any other person in Scripture. Yet there was a limit to how close Moses could come. In fact, God told Moses that no one could see His face and live (Exodus 33:20). How, then, can we see God? Colossians 1:15 describes Christ as "the image of the invisible God, the firstborn of all creation." Through Jesus, we can know the presence of God.

Read Hebrews 1:1–4. The author of the book of Hebrews began by reminding readers that God had spoken through the prophets in the past and now spoke through His Son—the Creator and His heir. Hebrews describes Jesus as the radiance of God's glory. "Radiance" comes from the Greek word for brightness and means "the radiance that shines from a source of light."[1] We see God's glory through His Son.

Next, the author described Jesus as "the express image of His person." This phrase is based on a Greek word that

---

[1] Enduring Word, https://enduringword.com/bible-commentary/hebrews-1/.

refers to a mark being stamped on something. *Expositor's Commentary* states this word has the same meaning as "man being created in God's image."[2] Through Christ, we see an exact, perfect image of God.

Preacher Charles Spurgeon explained the phrase this way: "Whatever God is, Christ is—the very likeness of God, the very Godhead of Godhead, the very Deity of Deity is in Christ Jesus."[3] In fact, when Philip asked Jesus to show the disciples His Father, Jesus replied, "Whoever has seen me *has seen* the Father" (emphasis added). Through Jesus, we can know God's nature, His holiness, His mercy, and His love. Because we've seen Jesus, we can see God.

Not only do these verses describe Jesus, they also tell us where Jesus is. He's now at the right hand of the Father, having reclaimed His position by God's side and above the angels. Although Jesus humbled Himself in death, He arose in completion of mission and rejoined His Father.

Reflect on the fact that Jesus is the radiance of God's glory and the exact image of God. How does that inform your understanding of God the Father and God the Son?

How does your understanding of God's presence and image in our lives affect your faith?

As you pray, verbalize your understanding of how Jesus perfectly reflects who God is.

---

[2] Frank E. Gaebelein, gen. ed., *The Expositor's Bible Commentary: Hebrews* (Grand Rapids, MI: Zondervan, 1981), p. 14.
[3] Charles Spurgeon, "Depths and Heights," https://www.spurgeongems.org/vols43-45/chs2635.pdf.

Day 36

The Depth of God's Love

For while we were still weak, at the right time
Christ died for the ungodly.—Romans 5:6

The theological term for being made right with God is *justification*. Becoming justified with God is not something we can do for ourselves. But becoming justified means that we are made holy and given the ability to stand righteously before God. Becoming justified also means that our sins are blotted out—they are wiped out as if they had never happened. David, in Psalm 51, entreated the Lord, "Wash me thoroughly from my iniquity, and cleanse me from my sin! For I know my transgressions, and my sin is ever before me.... Hide your face from my sins, and blot out all my iniquities." (vv. 2–3, 9).

Read Romans 5:6–10. What David longed for, Christ accomplished. Christ died for us, not because we are perfect or worthy, but because of His deep and abiding love for us. He didn't die for us because He hoped we would live better lives or because He saw potential that had been untouched. He died for us because of who we were. He died for us when we were weak—full of faults and frailties, full of self-righteous and self-centered plans for ourselves, full of our own personal desires for pleasures—and totally unredeemable.

Notice the phrase, "at the right time," in verse 6. Jesus died for us according to God's plan and God's timing. God's plan all along was to redeem the unredeemable, to save those who could not save themselves, and to love those who were unrighteous before Him. That plan was so important to Him that God willingly allowed His own Son—His one and only unique Son, the only one there would ever be—to leave heaven, come to earth to suffer and die for us. There is no greater love than the love God has for us.

When did you become justified through Christ? How has your life changed since then?

What is the worst thing in your life that you carry guilt for? Remember that through Christ's death on the cross, whatever causes you guilt has been wiped out from God's memory.

As you pray, meditate on this verse from the hymn "How Deep the Father's Love For Us":
>   How deep the Father's love for us,
>   How vast beyond all measure that He
>   should give
>   His only Son to make a wretch [like
>   me] His treasure.

Day 37

Our Mediator with God

For there is one God, and there is one mediator between God and men, the man Christ Jesus, who gave himself as a ransom for all, which is the testimony given at the proper time.—1 Timothy 2:5–6

In the Old Testament, the high priest was chosen once a year to go into the Holy of Holies and before the presence of God. He was chosen by the casting of lots, and before he entered the Holy of Holies, he had to make a sacrifice to cover his sins as well as the sins of the people of Israel. Hebrews 5:2 states that the high priest could "deal gently with the ignorant and wayward, since he himself is beset with weakness." The high priest's sacrifices were good, but they didn't last. Since the high priest was sinful, the sacrifice could never be perfect. The high priest served as a mediator who could come before God in the place of God's people. When the high priest entered the Holy of Holies, he represented the sins of the nation of Israel. And Hebrews 7:23 reminds us that each high priest served only once and then was replaced with someone else.

Read 1 Timothy 2:1–6. The role of the high priest changed when Christ became the one-time, perfect sacrifice. Since He was without sin, He alone could be the sacrifice for our sin. Jesus is the High Priest who can truly mediate between God and us.

The role of a mediator is to be the go-between for two estranged people or groups and to work to bring those two estranged groups together. One of the greatest things about Jesus serving as our High Priest is that He doesn't represent the sins of the nation. What Jesus did on the cross was personal—for you, for me, for each member of humanity. And because of His death on the cross and His resurrection, He can mediate between us and God for all of us personally. J. P. Sproul wrote, "As God, Christ brings divine justice and mercy to bear on our relationship to our Creator, and as man, Christ brings the perfect human obedience we need to be reconciled to God."[1]

> What does it mean to you that Jesus intervenes personally on your behalf?
>
> Why does it matter that Jesus continues to mediate between God and you, even after He covered the sin in your life?
>
> As you pray, meditate on Jesus' role as your mediator, and thank God for His plan to restore you to Him.

---

[1] J. P. Sproul, "Christ Our Mediator," at https://www.ligonier.org/learn/devotionals/christ-our-mediator/.

Day 38

The Mercy Seat in the Empty Tomb

And she saw two angels in white, sitting where
the body of Jesus had lain, one at the head and
one at the feet.—John 20:12

As a part of the instructions for building the tabernacle,
God told Moses to build a box or an ark. The directions
were detailed for building the box and then finishing the
box. When completed, the ark was forty-five inches long,
twenty-seven inches high, and twenty-seven inches wide,
and was made of acacia wood that was overlaid with pure
gold, both inside and out. The top of the ark was covered
with pure gold as well and had two gold cherubim placed on
it, one at each end. The the cherubims' wings were stretched
across the box to cover the top of the ark. God called this
the mercy seat and declared that He would meet the priest
there. Sometimes, the mercy seat was also referred to as the
place of atonement (Exodus 25:17–22).

Read John 20:11–18. Peter and John had come to Jesus'
burial tomb first and found it empty. When Mary Magda-
lene arrived just after them, she looked into the empty tomb
and saw two angels sitting on the slab where Jesus' body had
been laid three days before. Devastated, Mary asked where

the body of her Lord was, and when she turned around, He was there. Mary saw the risen Lord.

The angels on the place where Jesus' body had lain for three days are important. Where they sat brought the picture of the mercy seat on the Ark of the Covenant into the story and made the empty tomb the new Holy Place. Jesus, the ultimate atonement, had provided redemption through His death and resurrection. The mercy seat in the tabernacle and later the temple was no longer necessary as the place where God would meet the priest in the Holy of Holies once a year—on the Day of Atonement. Through Jesus' death and resurrection, His atonement for our sin happened once and for all. Because of His atonement, we have unrestricted access to God through the Holy Spirit—we don't have to wait to be allowed to come in His presence. Through the Holy Spirit, His presence is in our lives constantly.

Does the picture of the mercy seat in the empty tomb help you see the continuity of God's promises of a Messiah throughout history? Why?

How would your life be different today if you did not have unrestricted access to God? How would that change your relationship to Him?

As you pray, thank God that He gave you a way to receive atonement for your sin and access to Him.

Day 39

His Ascension into Heaven

And when he said these things, as they were looking on, he was lifted up, and a cloud took him out of their sight.—Acts 1:9

Luke wrote twice about Jesus' ascension into heaven. The first time is at the end of his gospel. In Luke 24, Luke very briefly described Jesus' ascension, giving as much focus to those who witnessed it as Jesus' leaving. However, Luke wasn't finished with his account of Jesus' ascension. He provided more details and context in Acts 1.

Read Acts 1:6–11. Jesus was taken up into heaven to sit at the right hand of God (Mark 16:19). Jesus left His earthly body behind as He went back to His place with His Father. Jesus left His earthly ministry and reclaimed His position as God.

In Jesus' leaving, He sent the Holy Spirit to be with His disciples, to dwell within them and to empower them to do the work He had called them to do. And the angels who appeared after His departure reminded those who stood gaping at the skies into which He had ascended that they would see Jesus again. Jesus would return again just as He had departed.

Interestingly, Jesus appeared to His disciples after His ascension to heaven. Stephen saw Jesus "at the right hand of God" just before his death as a martyr (Acts 7:55). Paul met Jesus on the road to Damascus (Acts 9:3–5). Jesus told Ananias to baptize Paul (Acts 9:10–19). According to Acts 16:7–10, the "Spirit of Jesus" changed the direction that Paul, Silas, Timothy, and Luke took on the second missionary journey. Jesus told Paul to stay longer in Corinth (Acts 18:9), and He appeared to Paul in the Temple of Jerusalem (Acts 22:17–18). Jesus stood next to Paul and told him to go be His witness in Rome (Acts 23:11). And, Jesus appeared to John on the island of Patmos (Revelation 1:10–20).

Jesus is the same . . . yesterday, today, and tomorrow. He cares about what happens in our world and in our lives, even from His exalted place in heaven. Jesus will return in the same way that He ascended into heaven. And, as believers, we are assured of spending our eternity in heaven because He lived, died, and rose again.

How do you experience Jesus' care and concern for you in your everyday life?

What would your life be like without Jesus' care and the presence of the Holy Spirit?

As you pray, ask God to help you see and understand the importance of Jesus' ascension in a new way.

Day 40

He Will Return in the Clouds

> Then will appear in heaven the sign of the Son of Man, and then all the tribes of the earth will mourn, and they will see the Son of Man coming on the clouds of heaven with power and great glory.—Matthew 24:30

In the Old Testament, God's presence and glory were often revealed through clouds. In Genesis 9:14–16, God put His bow (rainbow) in the clouds to show His promise of mercy after the flood.

In Exodus 13:21, God's presence in a pillar of cloud guided the Hebrews in the wilderness during the day, while a pillar of fire showed His presence at night.

Interestingly, Exodus 14:24 explains that these were not two different pillars, but one pillar with two different facets. Exodus 16:10 states that God's glory was revealed through the cloud. In Exodus 19:9, God told Moses that He would come before the Hebrews in a thick cloud so they could hear His voice. In Exodus 24:15–16, God called to Moses from a cloud. In the New Testament, God showed His presence at Jesus' transfiguration, coming in a cloud to acknowledge Jesus as His Son, and telling Jesus' disciples to be obedient to Him. These and many more statements in scripture are examples of a theophany—a visual manifestation of God to man. God showed His presence, His guidance, His mercy, and His glory visually through clouds.

Read Matthew 24:29–31. Jesus ascended in a cloud and He will come back in a cloud in the end times. This will be another theophany—this time a visual manifestation of the Son of God, who is God—to mankind. Jesus will send His angels out to gather His believers from throughout the world, and they too will be taken up in the clouds. This theophany of Jesus is no surprise. Daniel foretold it (Daniel 7:13–14) and Jesus revealed that it would happen to John (Revalation 1:7). Jesus' return will be earth-shattering, history-completing, and biblically fulfilling.

What God put into action with creation, what God's prophets foretold, what Jesus came to do in the first Advent, and what Jesus did for us through His death and resurrection will all come to complete fulfillment when He returns in the clouds. God's redemptive plan for His people will be complete, when the time is right and just as He told us.

In what ways do you think God continues to reveal Himself to His children?

What does it mean to you to see how God's redemptive plan throughout history will come to fulfillment?

As you pray, acknowledge the care and mercy God has shown to you through His redemptive plan that will be fulfilled completely when Jesus returns.

About the Author

Margie Williamson loves Christmas . . . the smells, the decorations, the food, the music, and those she gets to reconnect with over the season. She also loves writing devotionals and has done so for more than thirty years, along with writing Bible study curriculum. She and her husband currently live in the mountains where she is the Faith Editor and Feature Writer for NowHabersham.com, and he enjoys the outdoors.

If you enjoyed this book, will you consider sharing the message with others?

Let us know your thoughts at info@newhopepublishers.com. You can also let the author know by visiting or sharing a photo of the cover on our social media pages or leaving a review at a retailer's site. All of it helps us get the message out!

Twitter.com/NewHopeBooks

Facebook.com/NewHopePublishers

Instagram.com/NewHopePublishers

New Hope° Publishers, Ascender Books, Iron Stream Books, and New Hope Kids
are imprints of Iron Stream Media,
which derives its name from Proverbs 27:17,
"As iron sharpens iron, so one person sharpens another."

This sharpening describes the process of discipleship, one to another. With this in mind, Iron Stream Media provides a variety of solutions for churches, missionaries, and nonprofits ranging from in-depth Bible study curriculum and Christian book publishing to custom publishing and consultative services. Through the popular Life Bible Study and Student Life Bible Study brands, ISM provides web-based full-year and short-term Bible study teaching plans as well as printed devotionals, Bibles, and discipleship curriculum.

For more information on ISM and its imprints, please visit

IronStreamMedia.com

NewHopePublishers.com

**EXPLORE THE EASTER STORY IN
THIS 40-DAY DEVOTIONAL**